MY BOOK OF
Stories

write your own Fairy ~~Tales~~

BRITISH LIBRARY

First published in 2016 by
The British Library
96 Euston Road
London NW1 2DB

ISBN 978 0 7123 5642 8

British Library Cataloguing in Publication Data
A catalogue record for this book is available from the British Library

Designed by Perfect Bound Ltd
Picture research by Sally Nicholls

Printed in Malta by Gutenberg Press

MY BOOK OF
Stories
write your own Fairy Tales

BRITISH LIBRARY

Heartfelt thanks to my local Kintbury crowd for their unending support and encouragement.

I would also like to acknowledge the fantastic volume, *The Oxford Companion to Fairy Tales*, edited by Jack Zipes. It's full of wonderful and wondrous information.

Contents

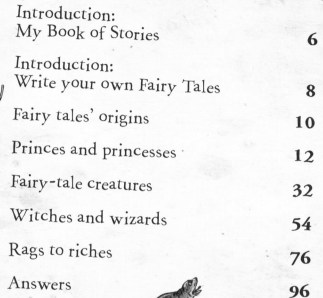

Introduction: My Book of Stories

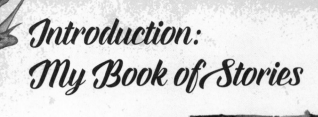

My Book of Stories is full of inspirational ways to start your own stories. Snippets of text collected from some of the best stories ever written such as *Cinderella*, *Romeo and Juliet* and *The Wonderful Wizard of Oz*, have been paired with story suggestions of how to write what happens next. Top tips on how to write a story, and lists of inspirational words used by expert authors such as Shakespeare, Lewis Carroll and J.K. Rowling, will help you along your way.

If you've ever read a book, but wondered what would happen if the hero decided to go left, not right, or wanted to give a minor character more to do, then this is the series for you.

On your story-writing journey you'll find fun puzzles to do, silly lists and titbits of information about authors and their books.

So you want to sit down and write some stories?

What do you need?

A pen, some paper, and then what?

You need to decide what to write about.

Where do you start?

Top 5 inspirational story starters

1. *Real-life stories*
2. *Myths and fairy tales*
3. *The world around you*
4. *A book that you've read*
5. *Your own interests, such as sport, music, or films*

Ready to get scribbling??

Introduction:
Write your own Fairy Tales

Long, long ago, far, far away on
the other side of the world …
(*The Bunyip* by Andrew Lang)

Think of fairy tales and magical lands, princesses,
cursed princes and evil stepmothers conjured up
by the imagination. Fairy tales are stories where,
because of the presence of supernatural beings, almost
anything can happen. A wolf can have a chat with a girl
as she walks through a forest, a mermaid can sacrifice
her voice for human legs and a princess can sleep for one
hundred years.

There are dark sides to fairy tales too, as heroes often
begin a tale living in poverty and sadness, and witches
lie in wait to devour children. Once the hero has
overcome all obstacles and either found riches or true
love, or both, they find their happily ever after.

In this book you can become part of the fairy-tale
tradition as you take one tale to another level,
mashup your favourite character and enchanted setting,
and create new heroes and villains.

It is not uncommon for film-makers to look to fairy tales for inspiration for a new blockbuster. These days, however, they are more likely to add a twist to the tale than tell the more familiar, traditional story. See if you can guess the titles of the films described below.

A snow queen builds a castle of ice

A fairy curses the baby princess, Aurora

A princess is banished from her home to a place where there are no happily ever afters - real life

Top 5 fairy-tale beginnings

Once upon a time...

A very long time ago...

Long ago there lived...

There once lived a...

A long, long while ago...

Maybe you'll use some of these story starters when you write your own fairy tales.

Fairy tales' origins

There is, first, the old tale which long ago men told their children, and these children told their children. Thus it was passed on from father to son ...

(The Story and History of Dick Whittington from Stories of London by E.L. Hoskyn)

Andrew Lang

Andrew Lang, a Scottish writer, is famous for his Fairy Book series, which he began in 1889 with *The Blue Fairy Book*. The tales in this book were drawn from Scottish and English folk tales and mixed with fairy tales written by Perrault, d'Aulnoy and the Grimms. He followed this up with *The Red Fairy Book* (1890), *The Green Fairy Book* (1892) and finally *The Lilac Fairy Book* (1910). By the end his sources not only included European folk and fairy tales, but also those from as far afield as Brazil, Africa, Japan and America.

There is very rarely a single, definitive version of a fairy tale. Though many fairy tales were first written down over four hundred years ago, it's thought that some familiar tales, such as *Beauty and the Beast* and *Rumplestiltskin* could be thousands of years old. In their retelling, in different cultures and different languages, many fairy tales gained new endings, had clear moral lessons added, and certain characters were dropped or changed.

DID YOU KNOW?

In 1937 *Snow White and the Seven Dwarfs* was the first feature-length film made by the Walt Disney Company. The Disney versions of fairy tales, including *Cinderella* and *Sleeping Beauty*, often softened some of the darker aspects of the original stories and, due to their popularity, are now the most familiar versions of the tales.

Charles Perrault

Perrault was a French writer who lived in the seventeenth century. In 1697 he published his first collection of tales, *Histoires ou contes du temps passé (Stories or Tales of Past Times)* which included new versions of *Sleeping Beauty*, *Puss in Boots* and *Cinderella*, among many other tales which are still familiar to readers today. All of these stories were based on folk tales, which were popular in France at the time.

Hans Christian Andersen

Andersen, a nineteenth-century Danish writer, is famous for his fairy tales. The sources of many of his most famous fairy tales, such as *The Princess and the Pea*, *The Swineherd* and *The Wild Swans* were Danish folk tales, though he also used medieval European literature as inspiration for writing new fairy tales, such as *The Emperor's New Clothes* and *The Little Mermaid*.

The Brothers Grimm

In Germany, Jacob Grimm and Wilhelm Grimm, together the Brothers Grimm, collected more than 210 traditional folk tales, and produced the renowned collection, *Kinder- und Hausmärchen* (*Children's and Household Tales*). The collection was first published in 1812 and included the now popular tales of *Hansel and Gretel*, *Rapunzel* and *Rumplestiltskin*.

The Arabian Nights

Also known as *The Thousand and One Nights*, the tales in this collection have their origins in Indian, Persian and Arab cultures. The earliest surviving manuscript of about two hundred and seventy of the tales (270 nights) dates from around the fifteenth century, though there is some evidence that there were written versions of the same stories as early as the eleventh century. Antoine Galland, the first European translator of *The Arabian Nights*, added the tales of *Aladdin*, *Ali Baba* and *Sindbad the Sailor*, which he had collected between 1701 and 1717.

Living in France at the same time as Perrault, Marie-Catherine d'Aulnoy also rewrote French folk tales. She published two collections of fairy tales, *Les Contes des fées* (*Tales of the Fairies*, 1697-8) and *Contes nouveaux ou les fées à la mode* (*New Tales, or Fairies in Fashion*, 1698)

Princes and princesses

"Oh, what a handsome youth! Have you brought him from fairyland?"
The History of Dwarf Long Nose
by Andrew Lang

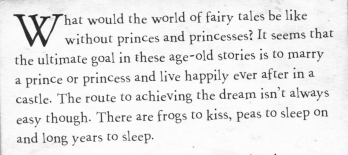

What would the world of fairy tales be like without princes and princesses? It seems that the ultimate goal in these age-old stories is to marry a prince or princess and live happily ever after in a castle. The route to achieving the dream isn't always easy though. There are frogs to kiss, peas to sleep on and long years to sleep.

In the pages that follow you'll meet a sleeping princess, a princess with a fish's tail, a prince that's been turned into a frog and even an ugly prince. Enjoy taking these royal characters on new journeys and creating some "happily ever after" endings of your very own. Perhaps in your stories the princess will be the heroine and rescue a prince in distress.

A real princess

The story of the *The Real Princess*, also known as *The Princess and the Pea*, by Hans Christian Andersen, raises a key question. What exactly makes a princess a real princess? In fairy tales she must be beautiful, but also kind, and importantly, in this one, be able to sense the presence of three peas beneath twenty mattresses and twenty feather beds! Perhaps anyone can be a prince or a princess if they have a good heart and a sprinkling of fairy dust.

List your top 5 favourite princes or princesses from films and fairy tales

1. ....
2. ....
3. ....
4. ....
5. ....

Time travel

"Is it you, my Prince," said she to him, "you have tarried long."

(*The Sleeping Beauty in the Wood* by Charles Perrault)

"you have tarried long" means "you have taken a long time"

Sleeping Beauty

In this well-known tale the princess pricks her finger on a spindle and falls into a sleep for one hundred years. Everyone in the castle, human and animal, falls asleep with her, and a briar thicket grows up around the castle, hiding it from view. One hundred years later, a prince hears the story of the sleeping princess and makes a bold attempt to pass through the thicket and enter the castle. His presence ends the curse and Sleeping Beauty wakes up.

One hundred years ago none of the things below existed. Can you imagine life without them?

mobile phones

space rockets

television

the internet

jet aeroplanes

What happens next?
Write the conversation between the prince and the princess as she wakes up and discovers that 100 years have passed. What new things does she discover?

The Frog Prince

But when the princess awoke on the following morning she was astonished to see, instead of the frog, a handsome prince, gazing on her with the most beautiful eyes she had ever seen.

He told her that he had been enchanted by a spiteful fairy, who had changed him into a frog. "You," said the prince, "have broken his cruel charm."

(*The Frog Prince* by the Brothers Grimm)

The Frog Prince

In this tale of transformation, a princess drops her golden ball into a spring and can't get it out herself. A frog then offers to get it for her if only she will let him eat from her plate and sleep in her bed. She agrees, never thinking that this will actually happen. However the next day, the frog comes to the palace door and reminds her of their agreement. Her father, the king, insists that she keep her word, so the frog eats from her plate and sleeps in her bed for three nights.

You have to kiss a lot of frogs before you meet your handsome prince, but why do princes get turned into frogs in the first place? Write the story of the prince in this fairy tale, including why and how he gets turned into a frog.

Ribbit, Ribbit

Have you ever thought about why the prince gets turned into a frog, not a dog, or a rat or a cat? Perhaps its because frogs look so different from their start in lives as frogspawn and then tadpoles, that the transformation to prince doesn't seem so far-fetched.

And they all lived happily ever after...

A sprinkling of fairy dust

A fairy who was at the birth of Riquet with the Tuft, and also the two princesses seven years later, gave these magical gifts to the ugly Riquet and the beautiful but stupid, Princess:

1. Riquet with the Tuft has the power to give great wit and intelligence to the person he most loves in the world

2. Princess 1 has the power to make the person she loves most incredibly handsome

Using the cast of characters below write a story about them that ends with the words opposite, which are from the fairy tale *Riquet with the Tuft* by Charles Perrault.

Riquet with the Tuft	has an "abundance of wit" but is "an ugly brat"
Princess 1	is "beautiful beyond compare" but has "no wit at all"
Princess 2	is "very ugly" but has "great wit"

"I wish, with all my heart," said the Princess, "that you may be the most lovable Prince in the world."

The Princess promised immediately to marry him, and the next morning their nuptials were celebrated.

Never judge a book by its cover

Have you ever been guilty of judging someone's character just by how they look? If you lived in a fairy tale and didn't give the frog, or the beast a chance, you might never find your true love! Some fairy tales teach us to look past a person's appearance to find the good character within them. Often these characters have been turned into something unattractive against their will. In these cases it's usually finding true love that lifts the curse, and in the world of fairy tales, unsurprisingly, the cursed character is most often a prince or princess.

Create your own prince or princess whose appearance has been changed by someone evil.

Prince or Princess ....

is turned into a ....

by ....

and finds themselves trapped in a ....

The only way to break the curse is ....

....

Draw a picture of your character

Top 5 princes and princesses in disguise

Beast from *Beauty and the Beast*
Donkeyskin from *Donkeyskin*
The swineherd from *The Swineherd*
The frog from *The Frog Prince*
Hábogi from *Hábogi*

Which one is your favourite?

Write your own story

Using the character you created on the previous page, write the story of how the curse gets lifted and their true identity is revealed.

_____
_____
_____
_____
_____
_____
_____
_____
_____
_____
_____
_____
_____
_____
_____
_____
_____

A royal test

There was once a Prince who wished to marry a Princess; but then she must be a real Princess. Princesses he found in plenty; but whether they were real Princesses it was impossible for him to decide.

(*The Real Princess* by Hans Christian Andersen)

Hans Christian Andersen's story, *The Real Princess*, opens dramatically. One stormy night there is a knock at the palace door. When the king opens the door he sees a girl who tells him that she is a real princess. The queen decides to put this to the test, so when she makes up a bed for the girl to spend the night in she places three peas on the bedstead, and then proceeds to cover them with twenty mattresses and twenty feather beds. The following morning the girl says that she had slept badly and thinks there must have been something in her bed. The queen and the prince think that only a real princess could have had "such a delicate sense of feeling", so the prince marries her.

Fast-forward twenty years. The prince and his princess are now king and queen, and their eighteen-year-old daughter wishes to marry a real prince. Write the story of her search for a real prince.

Questions to ask yourself before you write

Does she find a prince?
Are the potential princes set a test?
What qualities do you think a real prince should have?
Do her parents help?

Sea princesses

From the deepest spot in the ocean rises the palace of the sea king. Its walls are made of coral and its high pointed windows of the clearest amber, but the roof is made of mussel shells that open and shut with the tide. This is a wonderful sight to see, for every shell holds glistening pearls, any one of which would be the pride of a queen's crown.

(The Little Mermaid by Hans Christian Andersen)

Andrew Lang, a Victorian collector of folk and fairy tales from Scotland, wrote down the following lesser-known mermaid stories:

The Golden Mermaid
The Mermaid and the Boy
Hans, the Mermaid's Son

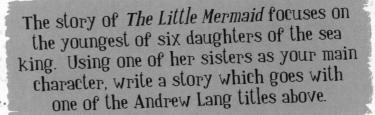

The story of *The Little Mermaid* focuses on the youngest of six daughters of the sea king. Using one of her sisters as your main character, write a story which goes with one of the Andrew Lang titles above.

✓ Title _____

Try using some
of these words
of the sea in
your story

deep
green
fish
calm
ships
dolphins
blue
iceberg
oysters
waves
seaweed

Write your own fairy tale of a prince or princess

In your story of princes and princesses will one of your characters be cursed? Will they be searching for love?

_____
_____
_____
_____
_____
_____
_____
_____
_____
_____
_____
_____
_____
_____

TOP TIP
Try setting your story in your home town and in the present day for a modern twist on a fairy tale.

Turn the page for more room to write

Can you unscramble the fairy-tale words in these anagrams?

CRESS PIN

☐☐☐☐☐☐☐☐

EAT BUY

☐☐☐☐☐☐

A DIMMER

☐☐☐☐☐☐☐

THE MOP REST

☐☐☐☐☐☐☐☐☐☐

BAT ANKLES

☐☐☐☐☐☐☐☐☐

RAY IF

☐☐☐☐☐

Fairy-tale creatures

Many authors today write stories about animals. Not only authors of picture books aimed at young children, but also stories aimed at older readers, including adults. Fairy tales are no different, and because the characters of fairy tales inhabit a world where almost anything is possible, the animals in fairy tales can do almost anything.

Most fairy-tale characters would like to have a creature on their side, preferably one who talks, and who is intelligent, and perhaps rather well dressed as well. Monsieur Puss of *Puss in Boots* is a prime example of a domestic animal who is helpful to his master.

Some other fairy-tale characters hope that the animal that they have come into contact with is actually a prince or princess. Then only have to find a way to break the curse to find their "happily ever after".

Then there are the animals which strike fear in even the most optimistic of fairy-tale characters. The wolf in *Red Riding Hood* for example, or perhaps any one of the three bears. These animals are also given human traits, such as the ability to speak or, like the three bears, set up home and eat porridge for breakfast. However, at any given moment, they might turn wild, and there is always the threat of being eaten by them.

In the following pages you will meet many of these fairy-tale creatures. Enjoy reading their tales and then creating new stories for them to star in.

"My name is Friend Wolf.
And where are you going thus, my pretty one, with your little basket on your arm?"
(*The True History of Little Golden-hood* by Andrew Lang)

List your top 5 books featuring animals

1. ....
2. ....
3. ....
4. ....
5. ....

The cat's the star

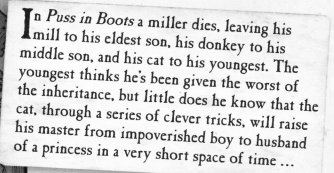

In *Puss in Boots* a miller dies, leaving his mill to his eldest son, his donkey to his middle son, and his cat to his youngest. The youngest thinks he's been given the worst of the inheritance, but little does he know that the cat, through a series of clever tricks, will raise his master from impoverished boy to husband of a princess in a very short space of time ...

"If you will follow my advice, master, your fortune is made; you have nothing else to do, but go and wash yourself in the river, and leave the rest to me."

The Cat's master did what the Cat advised him to, without knowing why or wherefore.

(*Puss in Boots* by Charles Perrault)

Write a new story for Puss in Boots to star in.

_____

_____

_____

_____

_____

_____

TOP TIP

Many modern adaptations of fairy tales combine characters from different stories together. Can you do the same? Maybe Cinderella is featured in your story, or perhaps the frog from *The Frog Prince*.

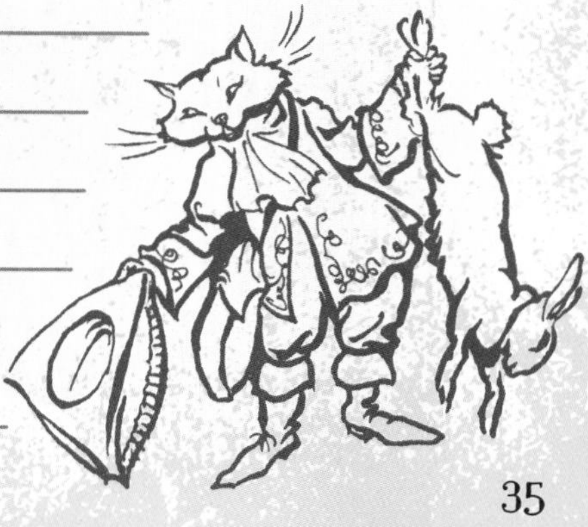

Rewrite a classic

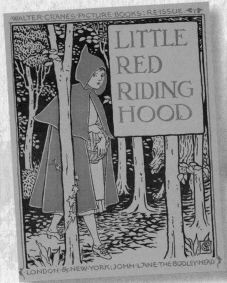

Like many fairy tales, the origin of the familiar tale of *Little Red Riding Hood* and the Big Bad Wolf lies in an oral tale. It was first written down by Charles Perrault, with many of the original elements changed, and published in 1697. The Grimm brothers also wrote a version, and added a new ending in 1812.

Write a new version of Little Red Riding Hood.

Characters

- Little country girl who wears a red hood
- Wolf
- Grandmother, poorly and bed-ridden
- Huntsman
- Mother of the little girl

Questions to think about before you write

Will Red or the wolf get to grandmother's house first?
Will Red survive?
What happens to the wolf in the end?

Beginning

- The girl is given some cake and wine by her mother, to take to her grandmother, and instructed not to stray from the path

- The girl is given some girdle-cakes and a pot of butter by her mother, to take to her grandmother

_____

_____

_____

_____

Set-up

- The girl meets a wolf in the woods and makes a bet with him as to who can get to her grandmother's first. She is distracted by the nature around her and takes her time

- The girl meets a wolf in the woods who persuades her to enjoy the nature around her on her journey, and encourages her to stray from the path

_____

_____

_____

_____

Problem

The wolf reaches the house first, devours the grandmother, puts on her clothes and gets into her bed

_____

_____

_____

_____

_____

_____

_____

_____

_____

Obstacle

The girl gets to the house, finding the door already open, and goes into her grandmother's bedroom, where this conversation takes place:

"Oh grandmother," she said, "what big ears you have!"
"The better to hear you with, my child," the wolf replied.
"But, grandmother, what big eyes you have!" she said.
"The better to see you with, my dear."
"But, grandmother, what large hands you have!"
"The better to hug you with."
"Oh! but, grandmother, what a terrible big mouth you have!"
"The better to eat you with"

The Brothers Grimm's ending

The huntsman hears the wolf snoring and, thinking it's the grandmother, goes in to check on her. He finds the wolf asleep wearing her nightdress and in bed, and realizes what the wolf has done. He cuts the grandmother and the girl still alive out of the wolf's stomach and fills it with stones, so that the wolf dies when he wakes up.

DID YOU KNOW?

The story of *Little Golden Hood* starts out as the same story, but the little girl's magical golden hood protects her, and the wolf is devoured instead.

Beauty and the Beast

Every evening after supper the Beast came to see her, and always before saying goodnight asked her in his terrible voice:

"Beauty, will you marry me?"

(*Beauty and the Beast* by Andrew Lang)

Write the conversation between the two characters in this picture

41

Out of the ordinary

He got out the tinder box, and the moment he struck sparks from the flint of it his door burst open and there stood a dog from down under the tree. It was the one with eyes as big as saucers.

"What," said the dog, "is my lord's command?"

(*The Tinder Box* by Hans Christian Andersen)

Have you noticed that most of the animals featured in fairy tales are actually quite ordinary beasts? Not the hybrid monsters of the Greek myths, or hideous vampires of Eastern European tales, but cats, dogs, frogs and horses are the kinds of creatures you are more likely to meet in a fairy tale. However, being in a fairy tale means that these animals are, in fact, far from ordinary. Meet Puss in Boots, for example, a savvy boot-wearing cat who is far more intelligent than his master. There's also the talking horse in *Goose Girl* and the frog in *The Princess and the Frog*, and not forgetting the three dogs in *The Tinder Box* with the first with eyes as big as saucers, the second with eyes as big as mill wheels and the third with eyes as big as the Round Tower of Copenhagen!

Create your own creature to star in a new fairy tale. What is your animal going to be like? Answer these questions to help you decide.

Is it a large or a small animal?

....

Can it talk?

....

Does it wear clothes?

....

Does it have magical powers?

....

Draw a picture of your animal here

TOP TIP

When choosing your animal think of the creatures you see in your daily life, from pets such as rabbits, goldfish and dogs, to farm animals such as cows and ducks, to the wildlife you see around you, from the smallest ant to the largest bird.

43

Write your own story

Write a new fairy tale starring the character you created on the previous page in which they help their master or mistress achieve their "happily ever after".

45

Microtales

Once upon a time there were three bears, who lived together in a house of their own in a wood.

(*The Story of the Three Bears* by Andrew Lang)

Starting with the sentence above, fill in the notepaper scraps with different microtales about the three bears.

What is a microtale?

A microtale is a very short story, with a beginning, middle and an end. It can be just a couple of words, or a few sentences long, but it must not be more than fifty words long.

In the well-known tale of *Goldilocks and the Three Bears*, Goldilocks is a young, fair-haired girl who steals into the house of Papa, Mama and Baby Bear. In the older versions of this tale, including Andrew Lang's *The Story of the Three Bears*, it is an old woman who breaks into the house of the bears. These bears are not members of the same family, but instead three bachelor bears, described as a "Great, Huge Bear", a "Middle-sized Bear", and a "Little, Small, Wee Bear".

TOP TIP
Every word counts in a microtale. Try to make sure you're not repeating any words unless absolutely necessary.

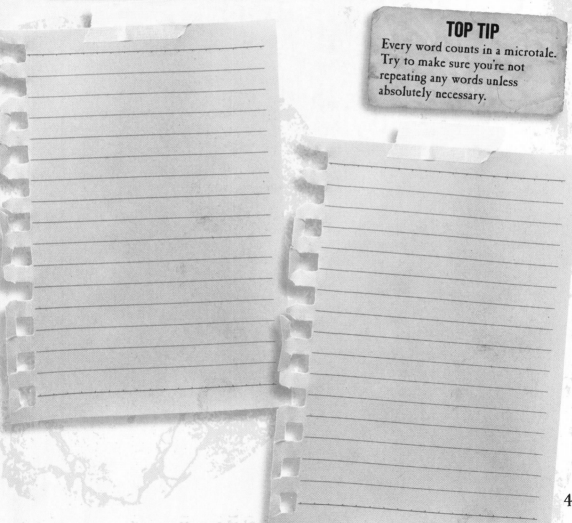

A tale of the unexpected

All of these elements exist, in some way, in *The Second Voyage of Sindbad the Seaman* by Richard Burton. Write your own fairy tale, using as many of these characters and settings as you can.

An idyllic island, abundant with fruits and flowers

An enormous bird, of gigantic girth and inordinately wide of wing, the roc

A roc's egg, a huge white dome rising high into the air

A desert island, with soil made of diamonds

A great serpent

An eagle

A merchant

Write your own story of strange creatures

Will the animal in your story have a master, or will they be master of their own destiny? Will they be the enemy or the hero?

Fairy tales, for all their strange and magical features, usually follow a simple story structure. Try planning your tale using this story mountain as a framework.

TOP TIP
Use a story mountain to help you plan your tale.

1. The Beginning - introduce your characters

2. The Build-up - set the scene

3. The Problem - what do your characters face?

4. The Resolution - how do your characters deal with the problem?

5. The Ending - is it a happy ending?

Give your brain a workout with this animal-themed crossword

Down
1. _____ and the 3 bears (10)
5. Baba Yaga's hut stands on these (4-4)
6. What type of animal knows where the Snow Queen lives? (8)
7. A prince was turned into what type of amphibian by a spiteful fairy? (4)

Across
2. The enormous bird in *The Second Voyage of Sindbad the Seaman* (3)
3. A dog with eyes as big as saucers features in which fairy tale? (3-6-3)
4. What type of animal did Little Red Riding Hood meet in the woods (4)
8. Fairy tale with a shoe-wearing feline (4-2-5)
9. Beauty and the _____ (5)

53

Witches and wizards

Witches have red eyes, and cannot see far,
but they have a keen scent like the beasts,
and are aware when human beings draw near.

(Hansel and Gretel by the Brothers Grimm)

Heroes and Villains

Most traditional fairy tales contain a hero and a villain. The villain can take many forms, from the Big Bad Wolf who is hungry for Red Riding Hood, to the giant at the top of the beanstalk, but more often than not, the villain is a witch, usually ugly, often cunning and persuasive. In some fairy tales their evil is hidden behind seemingly good deeds, such as those performed by the "funny little man", Rumpelstiltskin, or by the witch who places a tempting edible house in the woods for Hansel and Gretel to feast on.

Magic

Whereas fairy godmothers use their magic for good, to help the heroes achieve their dreams, witches and wizards use magic for cruel and selfish reasons. The pages that follow are full of clever tricks, ingenious disguises and fearful characters. If you're brave enough, turn the page and write your own darker fairy tales.

Top 5 fairy tales with "witch" in the title
The Witch and Her Servants
The Witch
The Witch in the Stone Boat
The Old Witch
Esben and the Witch

An evil trick

"Looking-glass, Looking-glass, on the wall,
Who in this land is the fairest of all?"

then it answered as before –

"Oh Queen, thou art fairest of all I see.
But over the hills, where the seven dwarfs dwell,
Snow-white is still alive and well,
And none is so fair as she."

When she heard the glass speak thus she trembled and shook with rage. "Snow-white shall die," she cried, "even if it costs me my life!"

(*Little Snow-white* by The Brothers Grimm)

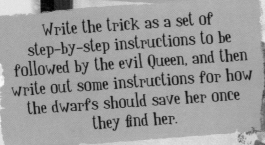

Devise a new murderous trick for the Queen to play on Snow-white

Write the trick as a set of step-by-step instructions to be followed by the evil Queen, and then write out some instructions for how the dwarfs should save her once they find her.

Each trick, such as persuading Snow-white to take a bite from a poisoned apple, that the Queen plays is in fact a deathly trap. However, each time, luckily for Snow-white, there is a way to escape death, whether the dwarfs save her or her prince comes to the rescue.

A witchy tale

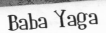

That whole day Vasilisa walked. She could find no path at all in the dark wood. But at evening she came all at once to the green lawn where the wretched little hut stood on its hens' legs. The wall around the hut was made of human bones, and on its top were skulls. The sight filled Vasilisa with horror, and she stopped as still as a post buried in the ground.

(Vasilisa the Beautiful and Baba Yaga retold by Alexander Afanasyev)

Baba Yaga

The "wretched little hut" belongs to an old witch grandmother known as Baba Yaga. She travels around in a great iron mortar and drives it with a pestle. She eats people as if they were chickens.

Magic Doll

Vasilisa owns a magical wooden doll, given to her by her mother when she died. When Vasilisa is threatened by evil or feels sad she takes the doll from her pocket, gives it a little something to eat or drink and tells it of her troubles. The doll is then able to help Vasilisa. Will the doll be able to help Vasilisa in your story?

What happens next?

Try using some of these fearful words in your story

devoured
wild
forest
smell
fire
sharp
locked
broom
hands
teeth

An evil enchantress

Rapunzel grew into the most beautiful child beneath the sun. When she was twelve years old, the enchantress shut her into a tower, which lay in a forest, and had neither stairs nor door, but quite at the top was a little window.

(*Rapunzel* by The Brothers Grimm)

Why does the enchantress lock Rapunzel away?

The original fairy tale doesn't tell us why the enchantress decides to lock Rapunzel in a tower where she can only be reached by climbing her long, strong plait of hair. Can you tell a story about the enchantress that explains her actions?

_____

_____

_____

_____

_____

_____

_____

_____

Questions to think about before you write

■ How do the enchantress and Rapunzel know each other?

■ Have Rapunzel or her parents wronged the enchantress in some way?

■ Is the enchantress jealous of Rapunzel?

In other versions of this tale the girl, known most often as Rapunzel, is blinded or turned into a frog. Can you add any other unexpected turns to the tale?

Create a wicked fairy-tale character

Column 1	Column 2	Column 3
Wicked	Dwarf	East
Venomous	Queen	Forest
Hobbling	Enchantress	Mountain
Old	Witch	Sky
Ice	Wizard	North
Grizzled	Sorceror	Rock

Take a look at the table above. To create your new character follow this simple template:

The .... of the ....

Insert word from column 1

Insert word from column 2

Insert word from column 3

Write a brief description of your character here.

Draw a picture of your character here

To help you find out more about your character, ask it some of the following questions

1. How old are you?
2. What or who do you care most about?
3. What's your biggest fear?
4. What one word describes you?

The evil queen in *Snow White* might have the following answers

1. I am twenty-five years old
2. My beauty
3. Finding someone more beautiful than me
4. Vain

63

Write your own story

Write a new fairy tale starring the wicked character you created on the previous pages.

TOP TIP

As you now know your character so well, consider writing your tale in the first person and from their point of view.

_____

_____

_____

_____

_____

_____

_____

_____

_____

_____

_____

_____

_____

_____

_____

The clue is in the song

The story of Rumpelstiltskin goes like this. A poor miller, who has a beautiful daughter, makes a boast to the king that he has "a daughter who can spin straw into gold". The king asks her to be brought to him, then locks the girl into a room full of straw and instructs her to spin it into gold by the following morning. He threatens death if she fails. Luckily for the girl, a funny little man appears in the room and offers to help her in exchange for her necklace. She agrees. The following day the same thing happens, and this time the girl swops her ring for the little man's help. The king is so impressed by the gold apparently spun by the girl that he asks her to be his queen, but only if she spends a final night spinning more straw into gold. The little man comes to her aid again, but she has nothing left to trade, so he asks for her first-born child. The king fulfills his promise and makes the miller's daughter his queen, but when the child is born the queen does not want to give it up to the little man. He says: "I will give you three days' time, if by that time you find out my name, then shall you keep your child."

"Merrily the feast I'll make.
Today I'll brew, tomorrow bake;
Merrily I'll dance and sing,
For next day will a stranger bring.
Little does my lady dream
Rumpelstiltskin is my name!"

(Rumpelstiltskin
by the Brothers Grimm)

Rumpelstiltskin's song gives his name away to the queen when one of her messengers overhears him singing it. Write a new song for Rumpelstilskin to sing which also includes his extraordinary name.

DID YOU KNOW?

There are other versions of this story in which different names are used, such as *Tom-Tit-Tot*, *Zorobubù*, *Titelli Ture* and even *Ricdin-Ricdon*. You could use one of these names in your song instead.

Good enough to eat

"Nibble, nibble, gnaw,
Who is nibbling at my little house?"

(*Hansel and Gretel*
by the Brothers Grimm)

Write a tempting description of an edible house, and then describes what happens when you are caught eating it by the witch who lives inside.

Think about including some of these words when describing your edible house, and don't forget to include your own favourite treats.

cakes
windows
sugar
roof
sweet
door
pancakes
chimney
apples
walls

Map it out

"She is no doubt gone to Lapland; for there is always snow and ice there. There it is, always glorious and beautiful!" said the Reindeer. "One can spring about in the large shining valleys! The Snow Queen has her summer-tent there; but her fixed abode is high up towards the North Pole, on the Island called Spitzbergen."

(*The Snow Queen* by Hans Christian Andersen)

Create a map of a place where a new fairy tale can be set.

TOP TIP

Base the place for this new fairy tale on somewhere that you know well. It could be your home town, or a beach, park or wood that you visit often.

Who lives here?

evil queens
wizards
witches
ordinary people
wicked stepmothers
princes
princesses
strange beasts
talking animals

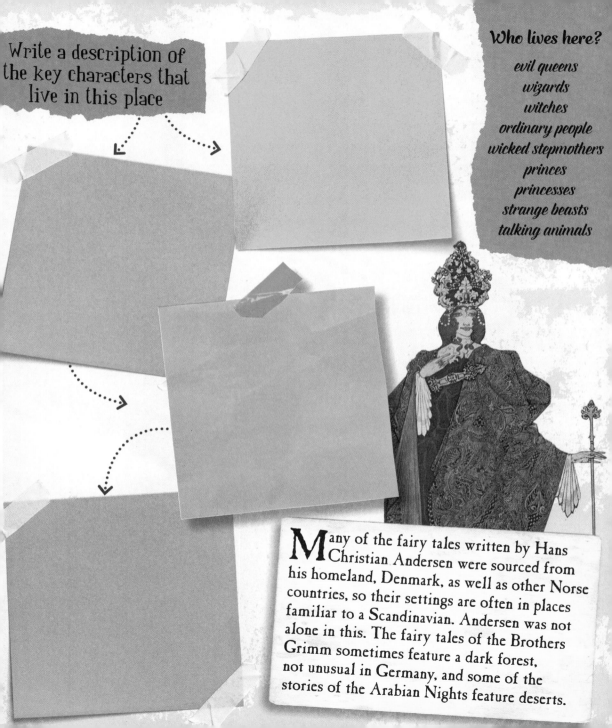

Many of the fairy tales written by Hans Christian Andersen were sourced from his homeland, Denmark, as well as other Norse countries, so their settings are often in places familiar to a Scandinavian. Andersen was not alone in this. The fairy tales of the Brothers Grimm sometimes feature a dark forest, not unusual in Germany, and some of the stories of the Arabian Nights feature deserts.

Write your own story of wickedness

Write a new fairy tale using the map and characters you created on the previous page.

TOP TIP
Before you write, take some time to research, and perhaps even create a scrapbook of your findings and your thoughts.

How to create a scrapbook

Stick in inspiring pictures from magazines

Make a note of interesting words and phrases

Doodle pictures of people and animals

Take note of books to read, films to see and music to listen to

Have a go at finding these enchanting characters in this tricky wordsearch

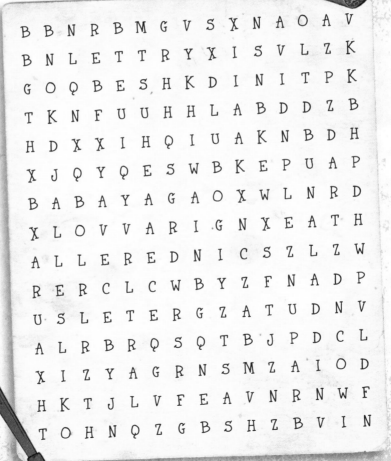

RAPUNZEL
SINDBAD
VASILISA
ALADDIN
SNOW QUEEN
BABA YAGA
GRETEL
ALI BABA
CINDERELLA
HANSEL

```
B B N R B M G V S X N A O A V
B N L E T T R Y X I S V L Z K
G O Q B E S H K D I N I T P K
T K N F U U H H L A B D D Z B
H D X X I H Q I U A K N B D H
X J Q Y Q E S W B K E P U A P
B A B A Y A G A O X W L N R D
X L O V V A R I G N X E A T H
A L L E R E D N I C S Z L Z W
R E R C L C W B Y Z F N A D P
U S L E T E R G Z A T U D N V
A L R B R Q S Q T B J P D C L
X I Z Y A G R N S M Z A I O D
H K T J L V F E A V N R N W F
T O H N Q Z G B S H Z B V I N
```

Rags to riches

The phrase "fairy tale" conjures up images of someone who starts a story unhappy, often living a life of poverty, or in the service of someone else. This person dreams of a better day when they won't have to work or worry where their next meal is coming from. By the end of a fairy tale, with a little bit of luck, and a sprinkling of fairy dust, the downtrodden hero's dreams come true.

Bounties of treasure can be found in the pages that follow, at the top of a beanstalk, at a magical royal party and in a secret cave. Each hero and heroine has a life-changing experience, sometimes with a little help from a fairy godmother or genie, but in other tales the hero makes his own luck. Enjoy reading these tales of rags to riches and then imagining your own fairy tale's happy ending.

Fill in the blanks

Here are the happy endings of the five fairy tales featured later in this chapter. Can you fill in the missing names?

.... served as Sheriff of London and was three times Lord Mayor.

He told his son the secret of the cave, which his son handed down in his turn, so the children and grandchildren of .... were rich to the end of their lives.

Thus .... took possession of the castle.

After this .... and wife lived in peace. He succeeded the sultan when he died, and reigned for many years, leaving behind him a long line of kings.

...., who was no less good than beautiful, gave her two sisters lodgings in the palace, and that very same day matched them with two great lords of the court.

Create a comic strip

Ali Baba and the Forty Thieves

The story of Ali Baba is included in most versions of *The Arabian Nights*, also known as *The Thousand and One Nights*. In this story Ali Baba, a poor woodcutter, observes a band of forty thieves, laden with treasure, entering a cave in the mountain by shouting "Open, Sesame!". When they leave the cave, they no longer have the treasure. Once they have left the area, Ali Baba decides to take a closer look.

Then Ali Baba climbed down and went to the door concealed among the bushes, and said: "Open, Sesame!" and it flew open.

(*The Forty Thieves* by Andrew Lang)

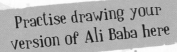

Practise drawing your version of Ali Baba here

Create a new comic strip which shows what happens when the cave door opens for Ali Baba.

Don't forget about the forty thieves! How will they fit into your comic?

A fairy intervention

In *Cinderella and the Glass Slipper*, the heroine suffers at the hands of her haughty stepmother and mean stepsisters. She is made to work as their servant, scrubbing floors and sleeping on a straw-bed in the attic. This all changes on the day the king's son decides to give a ball to which everyone will be invited. Cinderella's sisters work poor Cinders to the bone preparing their dresses, which leaves her with no time to prepare a dress for herself. She is resigned to the fact that she will not go to the ball. But in the moment of her deepest sorrow her fairy godmother appears...

DID YOU KNOW?

Cinderella's glass slippers weren't in the earliest versions of this famous fairy tale. In French the shoes were originally described as *pantoufles de vair*. *Pantoufle* means slipper, and *vair*, in old French, meant grey, or grey and white. Some people think that this means that the slippers were made from the fur of a grey squirrel.
The French word for glass is *verre*, so it's thought that some time before the story was first written down the word *vair* was misheard as *verre*, hence we have glass slippers in the version that we know and love today.

Her godmother, who saw her all in tears, asked her what was the matter.

"I wish I could –, I wish I could –," she was not able to speak the rest, being interrupted by her tears and sobbing. This godmother of hers, who was a Fairy, said to her:

"Thou wishest thou couldest go to the ball, is it not so?"

"Y–es," cried Cinderella, with a great sigh.

"Well," said her godmother, "be but a good girl, and I will contrive that thou shalt go."

(*Cinderella; or, the Little Glass Slipper* by Charles Perrault)

Has there been a time in your life when you wished a fairy godmother, or godfather, could have been there to help? Write a story about that time, imagining that a fairy helper was on your side and made a difference.

TOP TIP

Cinderella's godmother used the ordinary things she found around her to create the coach, horses, coachmen and footmen for Cinderella to go to the ball with. What ordinary things will your fairy godmother or godfather use magic upon to make your dreams come true?

What happens next?

After climbing higher and higher, till he grew afraid to look down for fear he should be giddy, Jack at last reached the top of the beanstalk, and found himself in ...

(Jack and the Beanstalk by Andrew Lang)

Continue the story from this point.

You don't need to be faithful to the original fairy tale of *Jack and the Beanstalk*. You can let your imagination decide where Jack is when he gets to the top of the strange ladder-like bean plant.

Words to
inspire you

wicked
meadow
giantess
wood
monstrous
harp
castle
fairyland
rock
giant
chariot
fairy
storm
peacocks

Fairy tale mash-up

Just as fairy tales bend the rules all the time, you can bend the rules too and mash up your favourite characters and story elements. This "Rags to Riches" chapter features *Jack* **and the** *Beanstalk*, *Ali Baba* **and the** *Forty Thieves*, and *Aladdin* **and the** *Wonderful Lamp*. Imagine if Jack found the Forty Thieves instead, or that it was Aladdin who climbed the beanstalk. Use the choices given below to create a brand-new rags-to-riches fairy tale.

Take a main character from Column A, and link him or her to one of the story elements from Column B

Jack	*and the*	Beanstalk
Ali Baba	*and the*	Forty Thieves
Cinderella	*and the*	Glass Slipper
Dick Whittington	*and the*	Cat
Aladdin	*and the*	Wonderful Lamp

Write your new story title here

.... **and the** ....

Choose some other elements from other familiar fairy tales to add to your new rags-to-riches tale.

poisoned apple
talking animal
witch
red cloak
long hair
fairy godmother
mermaid
dark wood
gingerbread house
castle

Now jot down a very brief outline of the new plot

Beginning

Build-up

Obstacle

Resolution

Ending

Authors draw inspiration for new stories from all sorts of different sources. Very often a book the author has read, or a film they've seen, or a piece of music they've heard might inspire a new character to be created, or a new plot to be devised. Fairy tales can provide this inspiration too.

.... *and the* ....

Write the fairy-tale title you created on the previous page here

TOP TIP

Have a look back at your plot outline before you start. As you are writing your story, read it out loud to yourself. Does your original plot still work? If not, go back to it and make some tweaks. Perhaps it simply needs a bit of magic added.

Write the fairy tale that goes with the title above.

A wishful conversation

"O my son, here is the lamp, but it is very foul." Then, taking a handful of sand, she began to rub the lamp, but she had only begun when appeared to her one of the Jann. And forthright he cried to her: "Say whatso thou wantest of me. Here am I, thy slave and slave to whoso holdeth the lamp." She quaked, and her tongue was tied, but her son hastened forward and said:

(*Aladdin and the Wonderful Lamp* from *The Arabian Nights* by Richard Burton)

What does Aladdin say to the genie? Write the conversation between Aladdin and the genie of the lamp in the speech bubbles opposite.

Questions to think about before you write

- What you would like to ask the genie?
- Would you immediately ask him to grant you your wish?
- Do you have any questions for him?

89

Big city dreams

One day someone told him that the streets of London were paved with gold. "Can it be true?" he thought to himself. "Is there so much gold in London that it is trodden underfoot? Am I not big enough and brave enough to tramp all the way up to London? Courage, Dick Whittington; off with you to London!" So off he set, and tramped all the weary way to the great city.

(The Story and History of Dick Whittington from *Stories of London* by E. L. Hoskyn)*

Write a present-day fairy tale about your journey to riches in the big city.

Answer these questions before you start writing.

Which city will you go to?

....

Does anyone or anything help you along the way?

....

How do you plan to make your fortune?

....

Will you be lucky, or will you have to work hard?

....

Write your own rags-to-riches fairy tale

_____

_____

_____

_____

_____

_____

_____

_____

_____

_____

_____

_____

_____

_____

_____

TOP TIP

A modern-day rags-to-riches fairy tale could be about a young person becoming a sporting hero, marrying a royal, forming a successful band, starring in a blockbuster film – what's your new fairy tale's ending?

Turn the page for more room to write

Answers

Page 9

A snow queen builds a castle of ice: **Frozen**

A fairy curses the baby princess, Aurora: **Maleficent**

A princess is banished from her home to a place where there are no happily ever afters - real life: **Enchanted**

Page 31

CRESS PIN
PRINCESS

EAT BUY
BEAUTY

A DIMMER
MERMAID

THE MOP RESTI
STEPMOTHER

BAT ANKLES
BEANSTALK

RAY IF
FAIRY

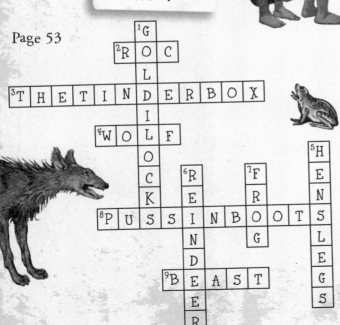

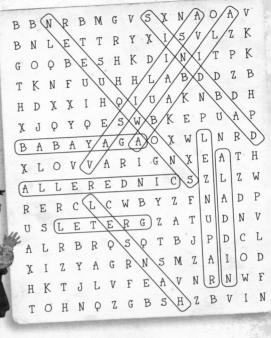

Page 53

Crossword answers:
2 (down/across) ROC
1 (down) G
3 THE TINDERBOX
4 WOLF
8 PUSSINBOOTS
9 BEAST

Page 77

Dick Whittington served as Sheriff of London and was three times its Lord Mayor.

He told his son the secret of the cave, which his son handed down in his turn, so the children and grandchildren of **Ali Baba** were rich to the end of their lives.

Thus **Jack** took possession of the castle.

After this **Aladdin** and wife lived in peace. He succeeded the sultan when he died, and reigned for many years, leaving behind him a long line of kings.

Cinderella, who was no less good than beautiful, gave her two sisters lodgings in the palace, and that very same day matched them with two great lords of the court.